P9-CAE-709

Houghton
Mifflin
Harcourt

Program Consultants

Shervaughnna Anderson · Marty Hougen

Carol Jago · Erik Palmer · Shane Templeton

Sheila Valencia · MaryEllen Vogt

Consulting Author · Irene Fountas

Cover illustration by John Shroades.

Copyright © 2017 by Houghton Mifflin Harcourt Publishing Company

All rights reserved. No part of this work may be reproduced or transmitted in any form or by any means, electronic or mechanical, including photocopying or recording, or by any information storage and retrieval system, without the prior written permission of the copyright owner unless such copying is expressly permitted by federal copyright law. Requests for permission to make copies of any part of the work should be addressed to Houghton Mifflin Harcourt Publishing Company, Attn: Contracts, Copyrights, and Licensing, 9400 Southpark Center Loop, Orlando, Florida 32819-8647.

Common Core State Standards © Copyright 2010. National Governors Association Center for Best Practices and Council of Chief State School Officers. All rights reserved.

This product is not sponsored or endorsed by the Common Core State Standards Initiative of the National Governors Association Center for Best Practices and the Council of Chief State School Officers.

Gus Takes the Train by Russell Benfanti. Copyright © by Russell Benfanti.

Printed in the U.S.A.

ISBN 978-0-54-453851-1

6 7 8 9 10   0868   23 22 21 20 19 18 17 16
4500617088   B C D E F G

If you have received these materials as examination copies free of charge, Houghton Mifflin Harcourt Publishing Company retains title to the materials and they may not be resold. Resale of examination copies is strictly prohibited.

Possession of this publication in print format does not entitle users to convert this publication, or any portion of it, into electronic format.

Unit 1

Around the Neighborhood 9

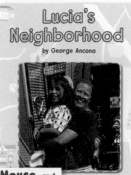

Be a Reading Detective!

Welcome, Reader!

Your help is needed to find clues in texts.
As a **Reading Detective**, you will need
to **ask lots of questions.** You will also
need to **read carefully.**

myNotebook

As you read, mark up
the text. Save your
work to **myNotebook**.

- Highlight details.
- Add notes and
  questions.
- Add new words to
  myWordList.

- Use letters and sounds
  you know to help you
  read the words.

- Look at the pictures.

- Think about what is
  happening.

Let's go!

UNIT 1

Around the Neighborhood

Stream to Start

❝ The more we get together, the happier we'll be. ❞
— Traditional Song

Performance Task Preview

At the end of this unit, you will write a story. You will be the main character! In your story, you will use details from a text you read in this unit.

hmhfyi.com

1

Channel One News®

9

What Is a Pal?
by Nina Crews

Friends Forever

🔍 LANGUAGE DETECTIVE

Talk About Words
Work with a partner. Use the blue words in sentences to tell about something you did.

myNotebook

Add new words to **myWordList**. Use them in your speaking and writing.

Words to Know

Read Together

▶ Read each **Context Card**.

▶ Make up a sentence that uses a blue word.

1 **play**

These pals like to play in the park.

2 **be**

They like to be on the same team.

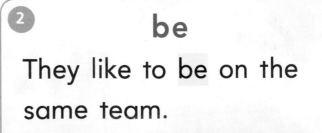

3 **and**

The children share the paper and paint.

4 **help**

These pals help each other wash the dog.

5 **with**

The boy was in a show with his pals.

6 **you**

I like when you play this game with me.

Read and Comprehend

Read Together

✓ **TARGET SKILL**

Main Idea As you read, look for one big idea that the selection is about. This is the **topic**. The **main idea** is the most important idea about the topic. **Details** are bits of information that tell more about the main idea. You can list the main idea and details about a topic on a web like this.

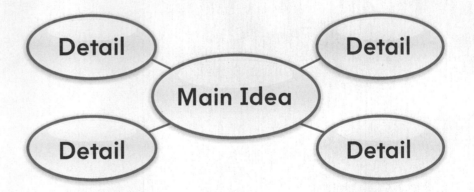

✓ **TARGET STRATEGY**

Summarize Stop to tell important ideas as you read.

Friendship

How do pals act?

Pals play together.

They help each other.

Pals take turns.

They are kind.

Pals have fun.

What do you do with your pals?

You will learn all about pals in

What Is a Pal?

💬 Think | Draw | Pair | Share

What is a good pal? Think about it. Draw a picture. Then tell a partner about your picture.

ANCHOR TEXT

What Is a Pal?
by Nina Crews

☑ **GENRE**

Informational text tells about things that are real. Look for:

▶ words that tell information

▶ photographs that show details about the real world

Meet the Author and Photographer

Nina Crews

Nina Crews comes from a very creative family. Her parents, Donald Crews and Ann Jonas, are both well-known artists. For her own artwork, Ms. Crews likes to make collages out of photos.

What Is a Pal?

written and photographed by Nina Crews

ESSENTIAL QUESTION

What is important about being a friend?

A pal can help you.

Sam and Nat can help Dan.

A pal can play with you.

Tad, Cam, and Nan can play.

A pal can be a pet.

A pal can be Dad.

A pal can be with you.

A pal is fun to be with!

Are you a pal?

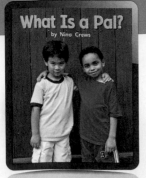
Dig Deeper

Read Together

Use Clues to Analyze the Text

Use these pages to learn about Main Idea and Informational Text. Then read **What Is a Pal?** again.

Main Idea

In **What Is a Pal?**, you read about what it means to be a pal. This is the **topic**. The **main idea** is the most important idea about the topic. What is the main idea? **Details** are bits of information about the main idea. What details did you find out about pals? Use a web to show the main idea and details.

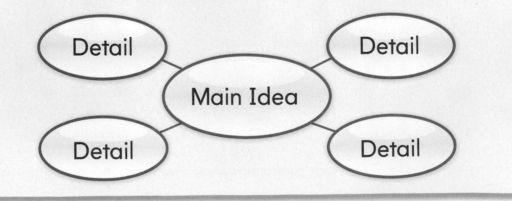

Genre: Informational Text

What Is a Pal? has details that are **facts.** Facts are true information. What facts do you learn from the words?

The pictures show real kids who are pals. What information do you learn from the pictures?

Your Turn

RETURN TO THE ESSENTIAL QUESTION

 **Turn and Talk**

What is important about being a friend? What details does the selection tell about being a pal? What else do you know about being a pal? Tell your partner. Speak in complete sentences.

💬💬 **Classroom Conversation**

Talk about these questions with your class.

1 Who could be a pal?

2 What things from **What Is a Pal?** have you done with friends?

3 What words tell about being a good pal?

WRITE ABOUT READING ··············

Response Read the last page of the selection again. Write a sentence to answer the question. Draw a picture to go with your answer.

Writing Tip

Read your answer. Add details to give information. Begin your sentence with a capital letter.

POETRY

Read Together

Friends Forever

☑ **GENRE**

Poetry uses words in interesting ways to show pictures and feelings.

☑ **TEXT FOCUS**

When words **rhyme,** they end with the same sound, like <u>blue</u> and <u>two</u>. Clap when you <u>hear</u> words that rhyme at the end of the lines.

Friends Forever

How can you be a good friend?
You can play with your friends.
You can share with friends and help them.

Damon & Blue

Damon & Blue
Just us two
Cruising up the avenue.
You strut, you glide
But mark our stride
Can't beat us when we're
  side by side.

by Nikki Grimes

Wait for Me

Wait for me
and I'll be there
and we'll walk home together,
if it's raining
puddle pails
or if it's sunny weather.

Wait for me
and I'll be there
and we'll walk home together.
You wear red
and I'll wear blue,
and we'll be friends forever.

by Sarah Wilson

Jambo

Jambo Jambo
ambo ambo
mbo mbo
bo bo bo
o o o
bo bo bo
mbo mbo
ambo ambo
Jambo Jambo
HI! HELLO!
Did you Did you
did you know
Jambo means
hello hello!

*by Sundaira
Morninghouse*

Respond to Poetry

- Listen to the poems again. Memorize some lines. Join in!
- Say more rhyming lines that could be added to one of the poems.

Compare Texts

Read Together

TEXT TO TEXT

Compare Friends How are the friends in the poems like the pals in the selection? How are they different? Make a chart.

Alike	Different
play	walk in
help	the rain

TEXT TO SELF

Write Sentences Write sentences to tell your classmates about favorite things you do with your pals.

TEXT TO WORLD

Describing Words Read the poems again. Find words that tell what the friends look like. Find words that tell what they see in their world and show how they feel.

ELA RL.1.4, RI.1.9

Grammar

Nouns Some words name people or animals. Some words name places or things. Words that name people, animals, places, or things are called **nouns**.

Read Together

Nouns for People

boy

dad

Nouns for Animals

dog

cat

Nouns for Places

house

sky

garden

Nouns for Things

book

door

bed

Talk about each picture with a partner. Name the nouns you see. Then write a noun from the box to name each picture. Use another sheet of paper.

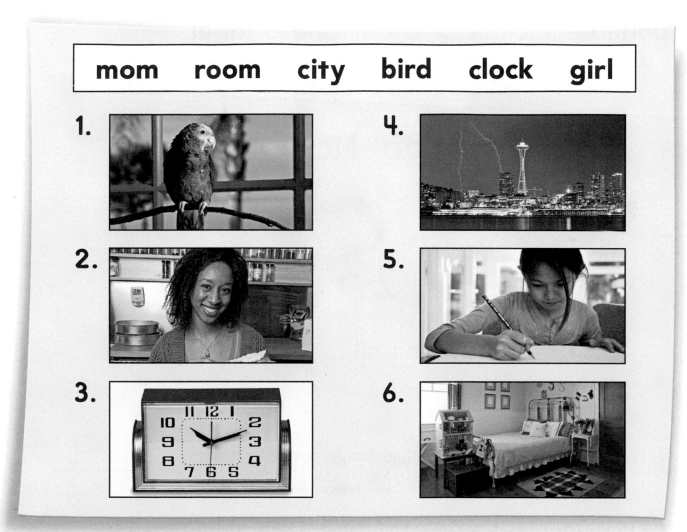

| mom | room | city | bird | clock | girl |

1.
2.
3.
4.
5.
6.

Connect Grammar to Writing

Share your writing with a partner.
Talk about the nouns you used.

Narrative Writing

✔ **Elaboration** Dan drew and wrote about his pals and what they do. Then he thought about what details to add. He added a picture of a ball and a **label**.

Read Together

Revised Draft

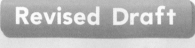

my pal Max

soccer ball

Writing Checklist

✔ **Elaboration** Does my writing have interesting details about my pals?

✔ Did I use nouns in my labels?

✔ Did I write letters neatly and correctly?

What do the details in Dan's writing tell you about his pals and what they do? Now revise your writing. Use the Checklist.

Final Copy

My Pals

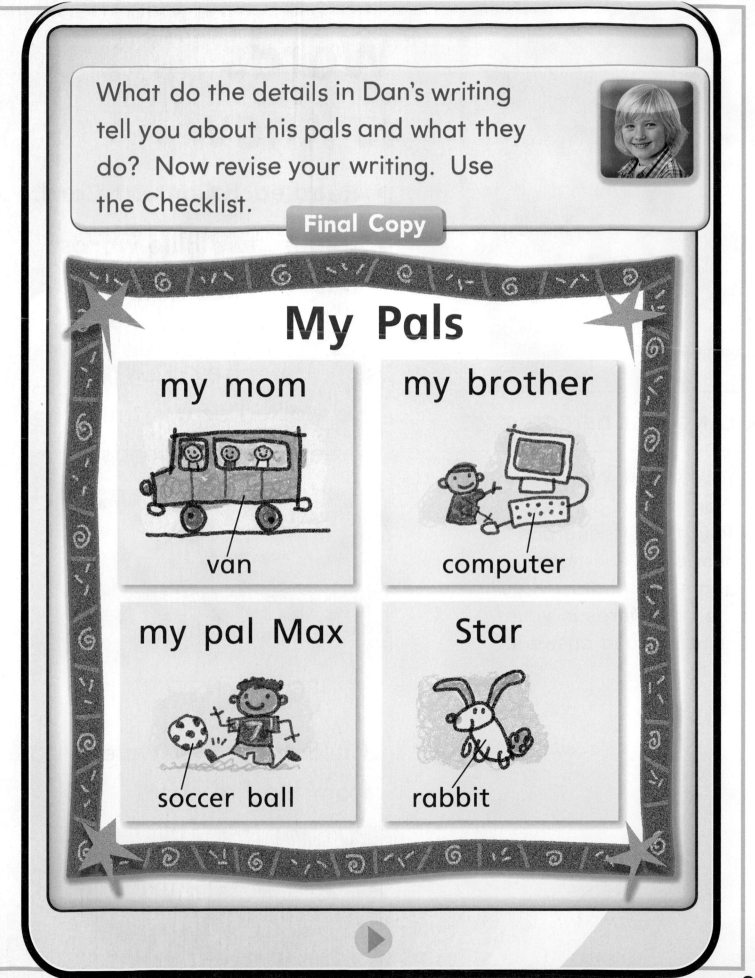

my mom

van

my brother

computer

my pal Max

soccer ball

Star

rabbit

Lesson

2

The Storm
by Raúl Colón

Storms!

Q **LANGUAGE DETECTIVE**

Talk About Words
Work with a partner.
Take turns asking and
answering questions
about the photos. Use
the blue words in your
questions and answers.

Words to Know

Read Together

▶ Read each **Context Card**.

▶ Choose two blue words.
Use them in sentences.

1 **he**
He walked across the
street with his friends.

2 **look**
Children look at water
from the fire hose.

3 have

We have fun seeing the fast fire truck.

4 for

The doctor had a kind smile for Ann.

5 too

They took hats and the sunblock, too.

6 what

What do people do to help you feel safe?

The Storm
by Raúl Colón

Read and Comprehend

☑ **TARGET SKILL**

Understanding Characters The people and animals in a story are the **characters**. Think about who the characters are and what they do. Use story clues, called **text evidence**, to figure out how characters feel and why they act as they do. You can write text evidence in a chart like this.

Characters	Actions

☑ **TARGET STRATEGY**

Infer/Predict Use text evidence to figure out more about the story and to think of what might happen next.

Weather

How can you tell a storm is coming?

Look at the sky.

Clouds move closer.

What might you hear?

Thunder crashes.

The storm is on its way!

There is some bad weather in the story you will read called **The Storm.**

💬 Talk About It

What do you know about storms? What would you like to know? Share your ideas with the class. What did you learn from others?

- ▸ Take turns speaking.
- ▸ Listen carefully.
- ▸ Ask questions.
- ▸ Answer questions.

ANCHOR TEXT

The Storm
by Raúl Colón

✓ **GENRE**

Realistic fiction is a made-up story that could happen in real life. Look for:

► things that could really happen

► people who act like people in real life

Meet the Author and Illustrator

Raúl Colón

As a little boy in Puerto Rico, Raúl Colón was often very sick. He spent a lot of time inside, drawing. He even made his own comic books. Today, Mr. Colón lives in New York and works as an artist and a writer.

The Storm

written and illustrated
by Raúl Colón

Pop has come in.
Look! He is wet.

Tim and Rip ran to him.

Tim, Rip, and Pop have fun.

Tim had to go to bed.

What did Tim and Rip see?

Tim hid in his bed!
Rip hid, too!

Look what Pop had for Tim.
Tim had a sip.

Pop had a hug for Tim.
He had a hug for Rip, too.

Pop sat with Tim and Rip.

Dig Deeper

Use Clues to Analyze the Text

Use these pages to learn more about Understanding Characters and Realistic Fiction. Then read **The Storm** again.

Understanding Characters

In **The Storm**, you read about different **characters.** What important things do the characters do? What does this text evidence tell you about what they are like? Use a chart to list the characters and their actions to help you understand them better.

Characters	Actions

Genre: Realistic Fiction

The Storm is a story with a beginning, middle, and end. It is a made-up story, but it could happen in real life.

In **realistic fiction**, characters act like real people. The events could really happen. Think about what happens in **The Storm.** Could it happen to you?

Your Turn

RETURN TO THE ESSENTIAL QUESTION

 **What happens during a storm?** Talk about what happens during different parts in **The Storm** and how it makes Tim feel. Use words and actions to act out his feelings in a group.

Classroom Conversation

Talk about these questions with your class.

1. How does Tim show his feelings?

2. How does Pop help Tim?

3. What does Tim see and hear during the storm?

 ELA RL.1.3, RL.1.4, RL.1.7, SL.1.4, L.1.5d

WRITE ABOUT READING ....

Response Look at pages 48–49. Write words to tell how Tim feels. Look for text evidence. Use the pictures and the words on the pages to help you.

Writing Tip

Read your answer. Add words that give information.

INFORMATIONAL TEXT

Read Together

Storms!

☑ GENRE

Informational text gives facts on a topic. It can be from a textbook, article, or website. Look for storm facts as you read.

☑ TEXT FOCUS

Photographs show pictures of real things with important details. Use these photographs to find out information about storms.

Storms!

A storm is a strong wind with rain or snow. It may have hail or sleet. Warm, light air goes up quickly. It mixes with high, cold air. Look! It's a storm.

This is a lightning storm in Pampa, Texas.

Kinds of Storms

A thunderstorm has thunder and lightning. It can bring heavy rain.

A tornado is a strong, twisting wind. It is shaped like a cone.

A hurricane is a very big storm. It has strong, spinning winds and rain.

A dust storm is a strong wind that carries dust for miles.

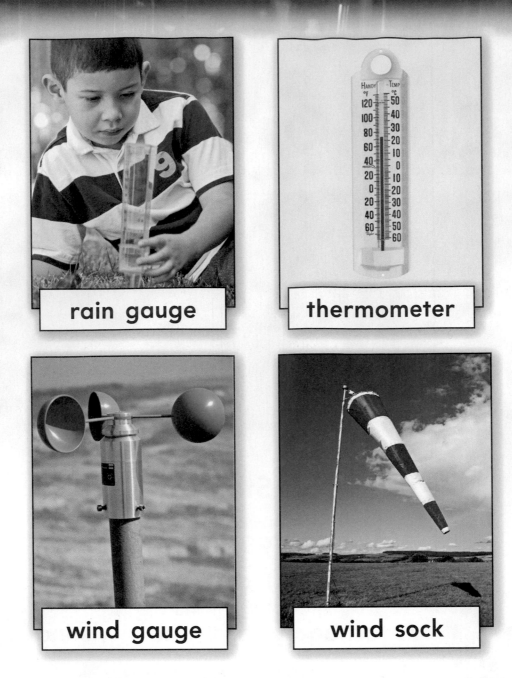

rain gauge

thermometer

wind gauge

wind sock

Measuring Storms

Scientists have tools for measuring storms. They measure heat and cold. They measure the wind. They measure rainfall and snowfall, too.

What storms have you seen?

Compare Texts

Read Together

TEXT TO TEXT

Compare Storms Look again at the selection **Storms!** Talk about each kind of storm. Which kind of storm did Tim and Rip see? Speak one at a time, and listen to everyone's ideas.

TEXT TO SELF

Write Sentences Write about a time you saw a storm. How did the weather change?

TEXT TO WORLD

Connect to Social Studies How can neighbors help each other in a storm? Draw a picture. Tell a partner about it.

ELA RI.1.9, W.1.8, SL.1.1a, SL.1.5

Grammar

Possessive Nouns Some nouns show that one person or one animal owns or has something. These nouns are called **possessive nouns.** They end in **'s.**

Read Together

Possessive Nouns for One Person

a man's hat

one boy's bed

Possessive Nouns for One Animal

a dog's ball

one cat's tail

ELA L.1.1b

Talk about each picture with a partner. Tell who has or owns something. Then write a possessive noun from the box to go with each picture. Use another sheet of paper.

| man's | bird's | boy's | dog's | girl's | cat's |

1. a _____ bike

2. a _____ ball

3. a _____ book

4. a _____ food

5. one _____ hat

6. one _____ nest

Connect Grammar to Writing

Share your writing with a partner. Say a sentence with each possessive noun you used.

Narrative Writing

my WriteSmart

Read Together

✔ **Elaboration** What did Kit's family do at the beach? After the trip, Kit drew and wrote about it. Then she thought of new details. She added a **caption** to explain her picture.

Revised Draft

We saw a fish.

Writing Checklist

✔ **Elaboration** Does my writing have interesting details about my family trip?

 Do my captions explain the pictures?

 Did I use nouns to name places or things?

Look for interesting details in Kit's final copy. Then revise your own writing. Use the Checklist.

Final Copy

Our Trip to the Beach

my family

a castle we made

We saw a fish.

We found shells.

Curious George at School
based on Margret and H. A. Rey's Curious George

School Long Ago

🔍 **LANGUAGE DETECTIVE**

Talk About Words
Work with a partner. Say new sentences with the blue words. Have the sentences tell more about the photos.

Words to Know

Read Together

▶ Read each **Context Card**.

▶ Ask a question that uses one of the blue words.

1 **sing**

These children sing with the music teacher.

2 **do**

The school principal has many things to do.

3 **they**

They like to work together in class.

4 **find**

The librarian helps children find books.

5 **funny**

The art teacher drew a funny animal.

6 **no**

No, you cannot cross until the cars are gone.

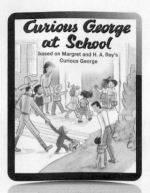

Read and Comprehend

☑ **TARGET SKILL**

Sequence of Events Many stories tell about events in the order in which they happen. This order is called the **sequence of events.** The sequence of events is what happens **first, next,** and **last** in a story. You can use a flow chart like this to write about the events in a story.

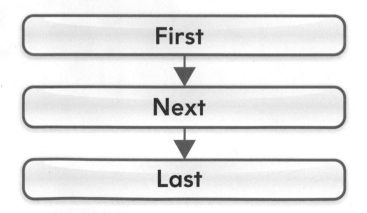

First

↓

Next

↓

Last

☑ **TARGET STRATEGY**

Monitor/Clarify If part of a story doesn't make sense, read that part again.

School

What do children do at school?

They read books.

They sing songs.

They paint and draw.

Children write letters and words.

Read **Curious George at School** to find out what happens at school.

Think | Pair | Share

What do you like to learn about at school? Think about it. Complete the sentences. Then share your answers with a partner.

I like to learn about ___.

___ is more fun than ___.

Learning about ___ makes me feel ___ because ___.

ANCHOR TEXT

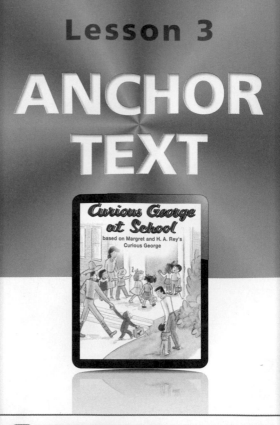

✓ GENRE

A **fantasy** is a story that could not happen in real life. As you read, look for:

► events that could not really happen

► animals that act like people

Meet the Creators

Margret and H. A. Rey

Children all over the world love Curious George! The Reys' books have been published in Spanish, French, Swedish, Japanese, and many other languages. Since the Reys wrote their first book about the curious little monkey, George has starred in more than 40 books, a TV show, and a movie.

Curious George at School

based on Margret and H. A. Rey's
Curious George

ESSENTIAL QUESTION

Why is going to school
important?

This is George.
He can help a lot.

George can sing.
He is funny.

He can see the paints.

Mix, mix, mix a bit.
Mix, mix, mix a lot!

It is a big mess!

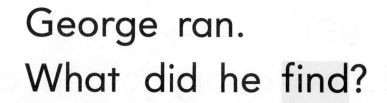

George ran.
What did he find?

He got a mop.
He had a big job to do.

No, no!
It is a big, BIG mess!
George is sad, sad, sad.

Kids help him do a big job.
They can help him a lot.
He is not sad!

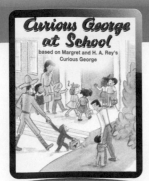

Dig Deeper

Read Together

Use Clues to Analyze the Text

Use these pages to learn more about Sequence of Events and Author's Word Choice. Then read **Curious George at School** again.

Sequence of Events

In **Curious George at School**, you read about what happens to George at school. Authors write what happens in a certain order. Think about what happens **first**, **next**, and **last** as you read. You can use a flow chart to show the order of important events in the story.

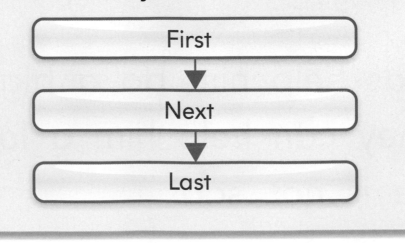

First

↓

Next

↓

Last

ELA RL.1.3

Author's Word Choice

Writers choose the words they use carefully. Some words help readers picture events. Some words tell more about a character.

The story says that George is funny. What other words does the author use to describe George and the mess he makes?

funny

happy

scared

Your Turn

RETURN TO THE ESSENTIAL QUESTION

Turn and Talk

Why is going to school important? Find text evidence that tells what George learns at school. Tell your partner what happens to him first, next, and last. What do you do at school that is important?

💬 Classroom Conversation

Talk about these questions with your class.

1 How does George try to help?

2 How do the children help George?

3 How is George's school like your school?

WRITE ABOUT READING ·

Response Write sentences to describe George. Tell what you think he is like. Use text evidence to give reasons why you think so.

Writing Tip

Use the word **because** when you write reasons for your ideas.

Read Together

School Long Ago

☑ **GENRE**

Informational text gives facts about a topic. This is a social studies article. Read to find out what the topic is.

☑ **TEXT FOCUS**

A **chart** is a drawing that lists information in a clear way. What can you learn from the chart on page 88?

School Long Ago

How did children get to school? Was going to school long ago different from going to school today? Let's find out! There were no school buses long ago. Some children had to walk far to get to school.

FROM THE PAGES OF
WEEKLY READER

WR

What did children bring to school?
Long ago, children did not have
backpacks. They carried their
things for school in their arms.
Children did not have a lot
of paper long ago. They
used chalk to write on small
boards called slates.

What did children learn?

Long ago, children learned reading, writing, and math. Some teachers taught children funny songs to sing. What do children learn in school today?

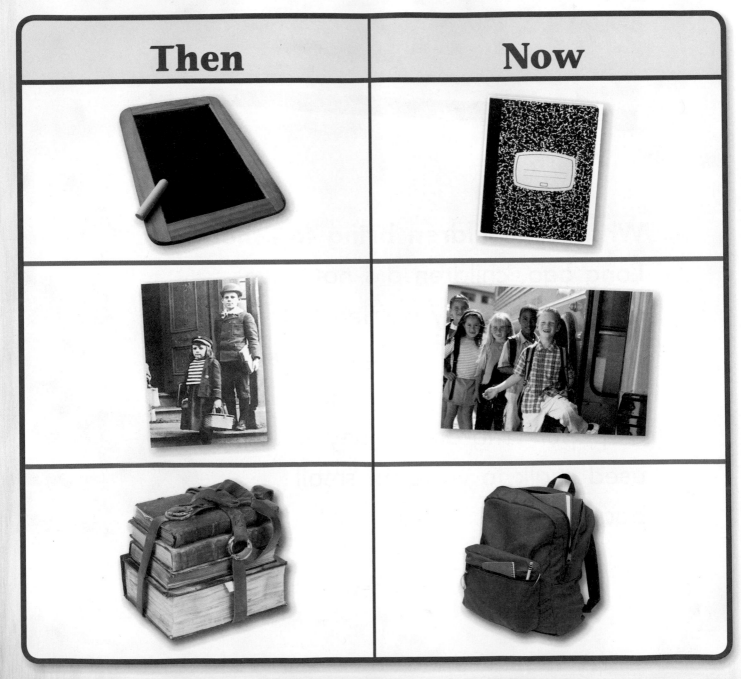

Then	Now

Compare Texts

Read Together

TEXT TO TEXT

Compare Genres Is the story about Curious George real or make-believe? How do you know? Tell how you know **School Long Ago** is true.

TEXT TO SELF

Connect to Experiences Think of something Curious George did that you have also done. Write about it.

TEXT TO WORLD

Draw a Map Draw a map of your classroom. Show where you sit. Describe your classroom to a partner.

ELA RL.1.5, W.1.8

Grammar

Action Verbs Some words tell what people and animals do. These action words are called **verbs**.

Read Together

hop

play

jog

hit

Write a verb from the box to name the action in each picture. Use another sheet of paper. Then act out one of the verbs. Have a partner guess the verb.

paint   help   sip   mix

1.

2.

3.

4.

Connect Grammar to Writing

When you revise your writing, use action verbs to tell about things you do.

Narrative Writing

✔ Purpose What things did Leah's class do one day? Leah wrote to tell about the activities her class did. She used action verbs to give readers a clear picture of the events. Leah changed **had** to an action verb that is more exact.

Revised Draft

read

We all ~~had~~ books.
         ^

Writing Checklist

✔ Purpose Did I write sentences about activities my class did at school?

✔ Did I use action verbs to tell what we did?

✔ Did I write letters neatly and correctly?

✔ Did I write an ending sentence?

Find sentences in Leah's final copy that tell about activities. Find action verbs. Then revise your writing. Use the Checklist.

Final Copy

Fun at School

We all read books.
We wrote stories.
Then we sang songs.
Today was a lot of fun!

Q LANGUAGE DETECTIVE

Talk About Words
Work with a partner.
Use two of the blue
words in the same
sentence.

Words to Know

Read Together

▶ Read each **Context Card**.

▶ Tell about a picture,
using the blue word.

1   **my**
The dentist will check
my teeth.

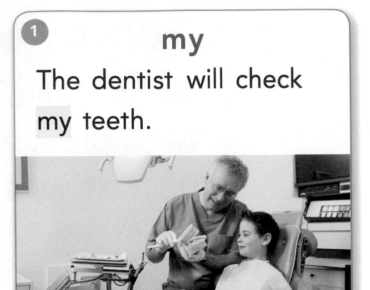

2   **here**
The firefighters keep
their trucks here.

3 **who**

Who brings the mail to your house?

4 **all**

The baker made all of these rolls.

5 **does**

Does this vet take care of dogs?

6 **me**

The zookeeper let me pet the koala.

Read Together

Read and Comprehend

Lucia's Neighborhood by George Ancona

✓ **TARGET SKILL**

Text and Graphic Features Authors may use **special features** like photos, maps, and drawings to explain a topic. Labels and captions can give more information about photos. Use special features to help you get information. You can list the features and the information you learn on a chart.

Feature	Purpose

✓ **TARGET STRATEGY**

Question Ask yourself questions as you read. Look for text evidence to help you answer them.

ELA RI.1.4, RI.1.5, SL.1.4, SL.1.6, L.1.1j

Neighborhoods

A neighborhood is where people live.
Neighbors are people who live nearby.
Neighbors help each other.
They are friendly.
How can you help your neighbors?
You will read about neighbors in
Lucia's Neighborhood.

💬 **Think | Write | Pair | Share**

What do you see in your
neighborhood? Think about
it. Complete the sentence: I
see ____ in my neighborhood.
Share with a partner. Act
out what you see.

ANCHOR TEXT

Lucia's
Neighborhood
by George Ancona

☑ GENRE

Informational text gives facts about a topic. Look for:

▸ words that tell information

▸ photographs that show details about the real world

Meet the Author and Photographer

George Ancona

What do you like to do for fun? George Ancona enjoys dancing, listening to salsa music, and spending time with his grandchildren. He does not like to watch TV or send e-mail. Mr. Ancona has written many books, including **Mi Música/My Music.**

35

Lucia's Neighborhood

written and photographed by George Ancona

ESSENTIAL QUESTION

Who can you meet in a neighborhood?

Hi! I am Lucia.
Can I get a goal?

Yes! We win.
We all get pins.

Bakery

What can Mom and I do?
Look what we get here.

Pet Shop

I can look at pets here.
It is fun.

Plant Shop

Mom let me get a plant here.
It is not big yet.

Who can fix the street?
Here is the man who can fix it.

10

Garage

Who can fix a car?
Here is the man who can fix it.

Who has on firefighter's pants?
They are too big to fit me yet!

Library

Does the librarian help me?
Yes!
We sit and look at my book.

My Home

Is it fun to be home?
You bet it is!

Dig Deeper

Read Together

Use Clues to Analyze the Text

Learn about Text and Graphic Features and Author's Word Choice. Then read **Lucia's Neighborhood** again.

Text and Graphic Features

In **Lucia's Neighborhood,** the author uses special features to tell more about the neighborhood. What information do the photos show? How does each label help you find and understand the information? Use a chart to tell about the special features and the information they give.

Feature	Purpose

Author's Word Choice

An author thinks about what words he or she will use. Choosing certain words or phrases makes the selection fun and interesting to read. Phrases like **on the ball** or **right as rain** are fun ways to say **perfect!**

As you read, ask yourself why the author uses the words he does. Think about what the words really mean.

Your Turn

RETURN TO THE ESSENTIAL QUESTION

Turn and Talk

Who can you meet in a neighborhood? Find text evidence in **Lucia's Neighborhood** to answer. Then draw a picture of a person from your neighborhood. Add a label. Describe the picture to your partner.

💬 Classroom Conversation

Talk about these questions with your class.

1. What words can you use to tell what Lucia's neighbors are like?

2. How is Lucia's neighborhood like yours?

3. What would you like to ask Lucia about her neighborhood?

WRITE ABOUT READING ....

Response Choose one place that Lucia visits. Write sentences that tell what the place is like. Use text evidence, such as the photo and the words on the page, to help you describe the place.

Writing Tip

Begin each sentence with a capital letter. End it with a period.

FABLE

Read Together

City Mouse and Country Mouse

City Mouse and Country Mouse

retold by Debbie O'Brien

Cast

Country Mouse

City Mouse

Cat

✓ GENRE

A **fable** is a short story in which a character learns a lesson. The characters in a fable are often animals.

✓ TEXT FOCUS

Fables usually end with a **story lesson**. The lesson is sometimes called a **moral**. Read this fable to find out what lesson the characters learn.

 Once upon a time, there were two mice.

 I love my country home. Come eat with me.

 I like city food better.

Come with me to the city.
We will eat like kings.

 I will come.

 Here is my home.

 Look at all this yummy food!

 Meow, meow. I will have mice for lunch!

 Who is that?

 It's Cat! Run and hide.

 City Mouse, my home does not have fine food, but it is safe. I'm going back to the country.

Compare Texts

Read Together

ELA RL.1.2, RL.1.9, RI.1.9, W.1.8, SL.1.4

TEXT TO TEXT

Compare Feelings How do Lucia and the mice feel about their neighborhoods? How do you know?

TEXT TO SELF

Respond to the Story What lesson does Country Mouse learn? Has anything like this ever happened to you? Write sentences about it.

TEXT TO WORLD

Discuss Neighborhoods Who or what makes your neighborhood special? Describe to a partner. Use details.

Grammar

Adjectives Some words describe people, animals, places, or things. These describing words are called **adjectives**. Adjectives can describe by telling size or shape.

Read Together

Adjectives for Size

tall

long

short

tiny

Adjectives for Shape

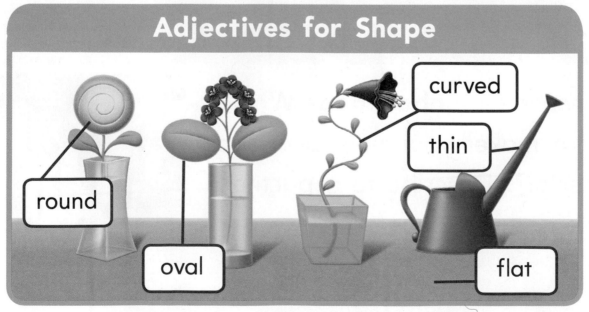

round

oval

curved

thin

flat

118

ELA L.1.1f

Think of an adjective for size or shape to describe each picture. Write the word on another sheet of paper. Use the adjective in a sentence.

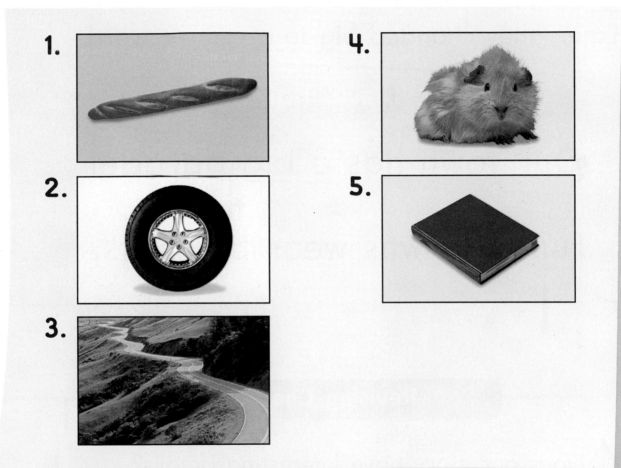

1.

2.

3.

4.

5.

Connect Grammar to Writing

When you revise your class story, look for places to add adjectives to tell what things look like.

Narrative Writing

my WriteSmart

Read Together

✔ **Elaboration** When you write a **class story**, choose interesting words that are just right!

Ms. Soto's class wrote about their town. Later, they changed **big** to a clearer word.

Revised Draft

Our town has a big parade.
                              tall
Funny clowns wear ~~big~~ hats.
                          ^

Revising Checklist

 Does our story have interesting details?

 Did we use nouns that are exact?

 Did we use adjectives to tell about size or shape?

✔ Did we write a sentence to end the story?

Read the story that Ms. Soto's class wrote. Find adjectives that tell about size and shape. Now help revise your class story. Use the Checklist.

Final Copy

Our Town Parade

Our town has a big parade.

Funny clowns wear tall hats.

A fire truck blasts its horn.

Horses prance down wide streets.

At the end, a loud band marches by.

Lesson

5

Gus Takes the Train
by Russell Benfanti

City Zoo

🔍 LANGUAGE DETECTIVE

Talk About Words
Verbs are words that tell what people and animals do. Work with a partner. Find the blue words that are verbs. Use them in sentences.

Words to Know

Read Together

▸ Read each **Context Card.**

▸ Use a blue word to tell about something you did.

1   many

There are many cars on the street.

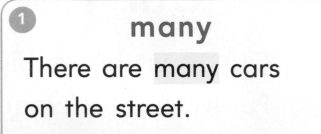

2   friend

She likes to ride the bus with her friend.

ELA RF.1.3g, L.1.1e, L.1.6

3 **full**

This train is always full of people.

4 **pull**

He can pull his pet in the wagon.

5 **hold**

She can hold her phone in her hand.

6 **good**

The ferry is a good way to see the city.

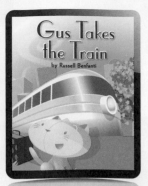

Gus Takes
the Train
by Russell Benfanti

Read and Comprehend

☑ **TARGET SKILL**

Story Structure A story has different parts. The **characters** are the people and animals in a story. The **setting** is when and where it takes place. The **plot** is the story events. It is the problem the characters have and how they solve it. You can use a story map to tell who is in a story, where they are, and what they do.

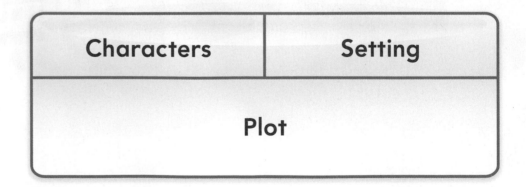

Characters	Setting
Plot	

☑ **TARGET STRATEGY**

Analyze/Evaluate Tell what you think of the story. Give text evidence to tell why.

ELA RL.1.3, SL.1.4, SL.1.6

At the Zoo

What can you see at the zoo?
There are many animals, like bears!
You can watch the monkeys swing.
You can hear the lions roar.
Which animal is your favorite?
You will read about a trip to the
zoo in **Gus Takes the Train.**

💬 Talk About It

What do you know about
zoos? Think about it.
Complete the sentences.
Talk about your ideas.
I know zoos are ____.
I would like to know more
    about ____.

ANCHOR TEXT

Gus Takes
the Train
by Russell Benfanti

✓ GENRE

A **fantasy** is a story that could not happen in real life. As you read, look for:

▸ events that could not really happen
▸ animal characters who act like people

Meet the Author and Illustrator

Russell Benfanti

If you like Russell Benfanti's colorful artwork, then visit a toy store. There you will find board games, toy packages, and computer games that Mr. Benfanti designed. "I love what I do!" he says.

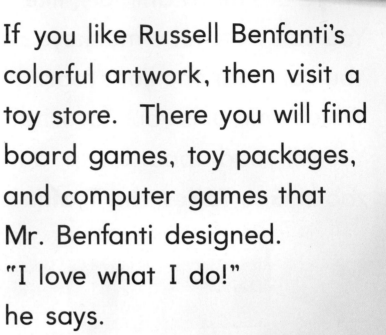

Gus Takes the Train

written and illustrated by Russell Benfanti

ESSENTIAL QUESTION

What happens
on the train?

Gus has to run to get the train.
He has a big bag to pull.

Run, Gus, run!

Gus cannot pull up his bag.
The conductor can help him.

The train is full.
Gus can see many kids.

Gus sat.

His big bag can go up here.

Gus met a friend!
Peg and Gus sing and play.

Peg can **hold** the cups for Gus.
They are too full!

Peg and Gus have a sip.
It is good!

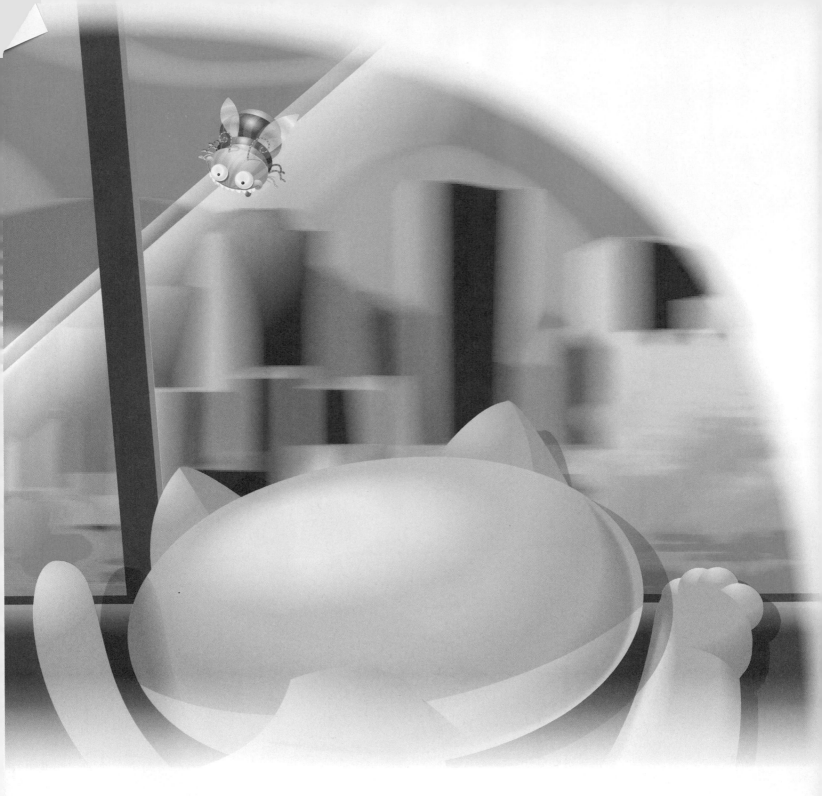

Gus can see a lot.
A funny bug is on the window!

We are here!
Gus had fun on the train.

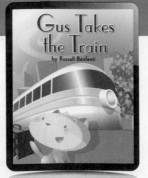

🔍 **BE A READING DETECTIVE**

Dig Deeper

Use Clues to Analyze the Text

Use these pages to learn more about Story Structure and Fantasy. Then read **Gus Takes the Train** again.

Story Structure

Gus Takes the Train has **characters**, **settings**, and a **plot**. All of these work together to tell the story. Who are the characters? Where are they in different parts of the story? Write text evidence on a story map to tell who is in the story, where they are, and what they do.

Characters	Settings
Plot	

Genre: Fantasy

This story is a **fantasy**. That means it is make-believe and could not happen in real life. In the story, Gus sings. Can cats sing a song in real life?

Look again at the pictures in the story. Do they look like real life? What text evidence tells you that this story is a fantasy?

Your Turn

RETURN TO THE ESSENTIAL QUESTION

Turn and Talk

What happens on the train? Tell what Gus does first, next, and last. Then draw a picture of something Gus will see at the zoo. Describe it. Show your picture as you talk to help explain your ideas.

💬 Classroom Conversation

Talk about these questions with your class.

1. Why does Gus take the train?

2. How does Peg help Gus?

3. Think about the end of the story. What will Gus do next?

WRITE ABOUT READING ··································  my **WriteSmart**

Response Write the story the way Peg would tell it. Write sentences to tell what happens at the beginning, middle, and end of the story.

Writing Tip

Add words like **first**, **next**, and **last** to tell when things happen.

INFORMATIONAL TEXT

Read Together

City Zoo

Informational text gives facts about a topic. It can be from a magazine, brochure, or website. What is the topic of this selection?

☑ **TEXT FOCUS**

A **map** is a drawing of a place. It can help you to get somewhere. A **key** shows what pictures on the map mean. What does each picture in the key on page 143 mean?

City Zoo

Welcome to the City Zoo! The zoo is full of many interesting animals. See if you can find all the animals on the map.

Key

tiger

elephant

polar bear

giraffe

We hope you have a good time at the zoo.

- Come with your family and a friend.

- Hold on to your ticket.

- Have some snacks.

- Pull a wagon.

- Take pictures.

Compare Texts

Gus Takes the Train *by Russell Benfanti*

City Zoo

Read Together

TEXT TO TEXT

Compare Selections Think about both selections. Tell which is make-believe and which is true. Tell how you know.

TEXT TO SELF

Give Directions Write to tell how you would get to one of the animals at the zoo. Then use the map, and show and tell your classmates how you got there.

TEXT TO WORLD

Connect to Social Studies Imagine that you are traveling to study animals. Where would you go? Find that place on a map or globe. Describe your trip. Use details.

Grammar

Adjectives Some **adjectives** describe people, animals, places, or things by telling their color or how many.

Read Together

Adjectives for Color

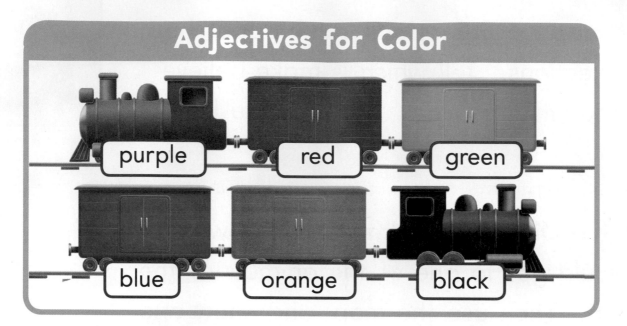

purple   red   green

blue   orange   black

Adjectives for Number

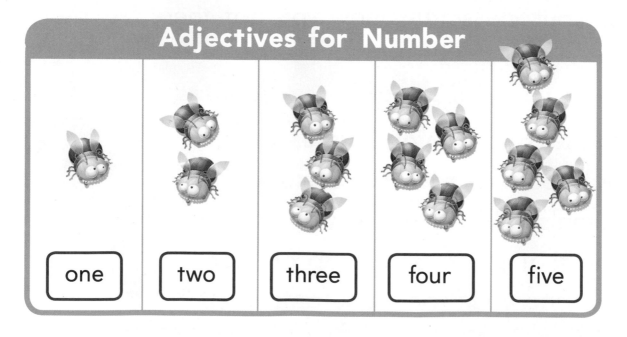

one   two   three   four   five

Write one number adjective and one color adjective to describe each item. Talk with your partner about how adjectives help tell what things are like.

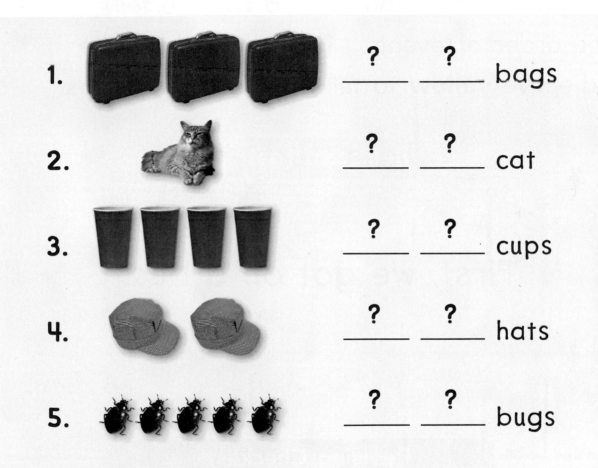

1. _____ _____ bags

2. _____ _____ cat

3. _____ _____ cups

4. _____ _____ hats

5. _____ _____ bugs

Connect Grammar to Writing

When you revise your writing, look for places where you can add adjectives to tell what things are like.

Narrative Writing

✓ WriteSmart

Read Together

☑ **Elaboration** When you write a **class story,** use adjectives to describe things clearly.

Mr. Tam's class wrote about a bus trip. They used **First, Next,** and **Last** to tell the order of events. Then they added the adjective **yellow** to tell more about the bus.

Revised Draft

yellow
First, we got on a⌃bus.

Revising Checklist

✓ Are the story events in the correct order?

✓ Did we use words like **First, Next,** and **Last** to show the order?

✓ Could we tell more by adding adjectives?

Read the class story. Find adjectives that tell more about the story. Find words that tell order. Now help revise your class story. Use the Checklist.

Final Copy

A City Bus Ride

Our class took a bus trip.
First, we got on a yellow bus.
Next, we sang two songs.
Last, we saw tall buildings and long trains.
We had fun on our class trip.

Write a Story

TASK Look at **Lucia's Neighborhood.** What would you like to do in Lucia's neighborhood? What places in the neighborhood would you like to see? Write a story to tell classmates about having fun in Lucia's neighborhood.

PLAN

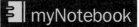

myNotebook

Gather Information Talk with a group about **Lucia's Neighborhood.** Where does Lucia go? What does she do?

Write your story ideas in a story map.

- Who will be in your story?

- Where will you go?

- What will you do?

Use the tools in your eBook to remember facts about Lucia and where she lives.

Characters	Setting
Plot	

Write your draft in *my*WriteSmart.

Write Your Story Use your story map for ideas. Follow these steps.

First

Begin your story. Who is with you in Lucia's neighborhood? Where do you go? Write a sentence that tells the first thing you do.

First, _____.

Next

What happens next? Write a sentence to tell about it. Use action verbs and adjectives to help you explain.

Next, _____.

Last

Write a sentence to tell the last event.

Last, _____.

Ending

Give your story a nice ending. Use one of these ideas or your own idea.

- Tell how your visit made you feel.
- Tell about the best part of your visit.

REVISE

Review Your Draft Read your writing and make it better. Use the Checklist.

Ask a partner to read your draft. Talk about how you can make it better.

- ✓ Is my story about how I have fun in Lucia's neighborhood?

- ✓ Did I use **first**, **next**, and **last** to show the order of events?

- ✓ Did I use action verbs and adjectives to help explain what happens?

- ✓ Does each sentence begin with a capital letter and end with a period?

PRESENT

Share Make a final copy of your story. Add a picture. Pick a way to share.

- Read your story to a group.

- Put your story in a class book.

Words to Know

Unit 1   High-Frequency Words

❶ What Is a Pal?
play
be
and
help
with
you

❷ The Storm
he
look
have
for
too
what

❸ Curious George at School
sing
do
they
find
no
funny

❹ Lucia's Neighborhood
my
here
who
all
does
me

❺ Gus Takes the Train
many
friend
full
pull
hold
good

B

bed
A **bed** is a kind of furniture for sleeping.
I sleep in my **bed**.

book
A **book** is a group of pages with words on them.
Frog and Toad is my favorite **book**.

C

car
A **car** is a machine with four wheels. We go in a **car** to visit my grandparents.

come
To **come** means to move toward something.
Maria called the puppy to **come** to her.

conductor

The **conductor** is the person in charge of a train. The train **conductor** watched the tracks closely.

curious

To be **curious** is to want to learn. Alan was **curious** about dinosaurs.

F

firefighter's

A **firefighter** is someone who puts out fires. A **firefighter's** job can be dangerous.

fun

To have **fun** is to have a good time. The children had **fun** playing tag.

G

George
George is a boy's name. My son's name is **George**.

goal
A **goal** is a score in a game. Anita kicked the ball and made a **goal**.

H

hi
The word **hi** means hello. I say **hi** when I see someone I know.

home
A **home** is a place where people or animals live. There are six people living in my **home**.

J

job
A **job** is work for people to do. Uncle Ned has a **job** in a store.

K

kids

Kid is another word for child. My uncle tells funny stories about when he and my dad were **kids**.

L

librarian

A **librarian** works in a place where many books are kept. The **librarian** helped me find the book I was looking for.

Lucia

Lucia is a girl's name. My sister's name is **Lucia**.

M

mess

A **mess** is something that is not neat. My sister's room is a **mess!**

N

neighborhood

A **neighborhood** is a part of a city or town.
Jim walks to the store in his **neighborhood**.

P

paints

Paints are liquids with colors in them.
Dip the big brushes into the **paints**.

pal

A **pal** is a friend. Benny is
my best **pal**.

pants

People wear **pants** over their legs.
Lucy's **pants** have two big pockets.

pet

A **pet** is an animal who lives with you.
My cat Sam is the best **pet** ever!

plant

A **plant** is anything alive that is not a person or an animal. We have a **plant** with big green leaves in our kitchen.

Pop

Pop is one name for a grandfather. I call my mother's father **Pop**.

S

school

A **school** is a place where students learn from teachers. I learn to read at **school**.

storm

A **storm** is strong wind, rain, or snow. Lots of rain fell during the **storm**.

street

A **street** is a road in a city or a town. We live on a very busy **street**.

T

takes

The word **takes** can mean to travel by.
Mia **takes** the bus to school.

this

This means something that is near you.
This is the book I'm taking home.

train

A **train** is a group of railroad
cars. This summer my family
is going on a **train** ride.

W

wet

Wet means covered with liquid. Juan got
wet when he went out in the rain.

what

The word **what** is used to ask questions.
What did you eat for breakfast?

window

A **window** is an open place
in a wall. Sasha opened
the **window.**

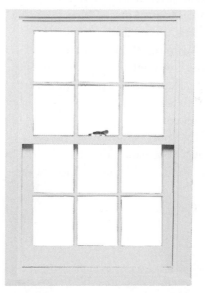

Copyright (c) 2007 by Houghton Mifflin Harcourt Publishing Company. Adapted
and reproduced by permission from *The American Heritage First Dictionary* and
The American Heritage Children's Dictionary.

Acknowledgments

Curious George at School, text by Houghton Mifflin Harcourt Publishing, illustrated by Margret and H.A. Rey. Copyright ©2011 by Houghton Mifflin Harcourt Publishing Company. All rights reserved. The character Curious George® including without limitation the character's name and the character's likeness are registered trademarks of Houghton Mifflin Harcourt Publishing Company. Curious George logo is a trademark of Houghton Mifflin Harcourt Publishing Company.

"Damon & Blue" from *My Man Blue* by Nikki Grimes. Copyright ©1999 by Nikki Grimes. Reprinted by permission of Dial Books for Young Readers, a division of Penguin Young Readers Group, a member of Penguin Group (USA) Inc., 345 Hudson Street, New York, NY 10014 and Curtis Brown, Ltd.

"Jambo" from *Nightfeathers* by Sundaira Morninghouse. Copyright ©1989 by Sundaira Morninghouse. Reprinted by permission of Open Hand Publishing, LLC (www.openhand.com).

"Wait for Me" by Sarah Wilson from *June Is a Tune That Jumps on a Stair*. Copyright ©1992 by Sarah Wilson. Reprinted by permission of the author.

Credits

Placement Key:
(r) right, (l) left, (c) center, (t) top, (b) bottom, (bg) background

Photo Credits
3 (cl) © Rommel/Masterfile; **3** (bl) ©Colin Hogan/Alamy; **4** (bl) © Douglas Keister/Corbis; **5** (bl) ©Underwood Archives; **5** (bl) ullstein bild/The Granger Collection; **5** (bl) Comstock/Fotosearch; **6** (bl) ©George Ancona; **6** (br) ©George Ancona; **6** (tl) ©George Ancona; **8** ©PatrikOntkovic/Shutterstock; **9** ©Pressmaster/Shutterstock; **10** © Ariel Skelley/CORBIS; **10** (b) © Ariel Skelley/CORBIS; **10** (tl) © Rommel/Masterfile; **10** (tc) ©Colin Hogan/Alamy; **11** (tl) ©Bob Krist/Corbis; **11** (tr) Ariel Skelley/CORBIS; **11** (br) ©Paul Austring Photography/First Light/Getty Images; **11** (bl) ©Dirk Anschutz/Stone/Getty Images; **13** ©Brand X Pictures/Getty Images; **14** © Rommel/Masterfile; **15** (t) © Rommel/Masterfile; **26** © Rommel/Masterfile; **27** © Rommel/Masterfile; **28** Ryan McVey/Photodisc/Getty Images; **29** © Rommel/Masterfile; **30** © Heide Benser/Corbis; **30** ©Colin Hogan/Alamy; **32** ©Colin Hogan/Alamy; **32** ©Colin Hogan/Alamy; **33** (tl) © Rommel/Masterfile; **33** ©Colin Hogan/Alamy; **34** (cl) © Photodisc / Alamy; **34** (bl) ©Juniors Bildarchiv/Alamy; **35** (tl) © Julian Winslow/Corbis; **35** (bl) ©Rachel Watson/Stone/Getty Images; **35** (cr) © Look Photography/Beateworks/Corbis; **35** (bl) © Patrick Bennett/CORBIS; **35** Corbis; **38** (br) © Nancy G Fire Photography, Nancy Greifenhagen/Alamy Images; **38** (t) ©Amy Etra/PhotoEdit; **38** (tc) © Douglas Keister/Corbis; **39** (cr) ©Jupiter Images/Comstock Images/Alamy; **39** (tr) ©Thomas Barwick/Riser/Getty Images; **39** (tl) ©Sascha Pflaeging/Riser/Getty Images; **39** (cl) ©Richard Hutchings/PhotoEdit; **40** Corbis; **55** Ryan McGinnis/Flickr/Getty Images; **57** Bananastock/Jupiterimages/Getty Images; **58** (c) © Douglas Keister/Corbis; **58** © Douglas Keister/Corbis; **60** (tr) ©comstock/Getty Images; **60** (c) ©Photodisc/Don Farrall, Lightworks Studio/Getty Images; **60** (cr) © Authors Image / Alamy; **60** (tl) © David Young-Wolff / PhotoEdit; **60** (bl) © matthiasengelien.com/Alamy; **61** ©Kenneth Langford/Corbis; **61** (b) ©GlowImages/Alamy; **61** © Douglas Keister/Corbis; **66** (c) © Michael

Newman / PhotoEdit; **66** (tc) ©Underwood Archives; **66** (tc) ullstein bild / The Granger Collection; **66** (tc) Comstock/Fotosearch; **67** (tl) ©Stuart Pearce/Age FotoStock; **67** (br) © Getty Images Royalty Free; **67** (tr) Comstock/Getty Images; **68** JUPITERIMAGES/ BananaStock / Alamy; **85** Digital Vision/Getty Images; **86** (b) ©Underwood Archives; **86** (tl) ©Underwood Archives; **86** (tl) ullstein bild / The Granger Collection; **86** (tl) Comstock/Fotosearch; **87** (tc) ullstein bild / The Granger Collection; **87** (tl) Comstock/Fotosearch; **88** (tr) ©Corbis; **88** (r) Comstock/Fotosearch; **88** (cr) Brand X Pictures/ fotosearch.com; **88** (bl) © JUPITERIMAGES/ PHOTOS.COM / Alamy; **88** (br) PhotoDisc/ Getty Images; **88** (cl) ©Underwood Archives; **89** (cr) ©OJO Images/Getty Images; **89** (tl) ©Underwood Archives; **89** (tl) ullstein bild / The Granger Collection; **89** (tl) Comstock/ Fotosearch; **94** (tc) © Kelly Redinger/Design Pics/Corbis; **94** (b) ©Richard Hamilton Smith/ Corbis; **94** (tl) ©George Ancona; **95** (cr) LOOK Die Bildagentur der Fotografen GmbH/Alamy; **95** (tl) © Michael Macor/San Francisco Chronicle/ Corbis; **95** (bl) © Corbis; **95** (tr) ©Andersen Ross/ Digital Vision/Getty Images; **96** (tl) ©George Ancona; **97** (bg) Jupiterimages/Getty Images; **98** (cr) ©George Ancona; **98** (tl) ©George Ancona; **99** (b) ©George Ancona; **100** ©George Ancona; **101** ©George Ancona; **102** ©George Ancona; **103** ©George Ancona; **104** ©George Ancona; **105** ©George Ancona; **106** ©George Ancona; **107** ©George Ancona; **108** ©George Ancona; **109** ©George Ancona; **110** (tl) ©George Ancona; **111** (b) © David Buffington\Getty Images; **112** (br) C Squared Studios/Photodisc/Getty Images; **113** (tr) ©George Ancona; **117** (tc) ©George Ancona; **119** (bl) ©Chad Ehlers/Photographer's Choice/Getty Images; **119** (cl) BrandXpictures/ Burke/Triolo; **119** (tr) ©PhotoDisc/Getty Images; **119** (tl) ©Image Idea/Fotosearch; **122** (bc) © Michael Newman / PhotoEdit; **122** (c) ©Mitchell Funk/Photographer's Choice/Getty Images; **123** (cl) ©Veer; **123** (tl) © Digital Vision Ltd. / SuperStock; **123** (tr) © Michael Newman/ PhotoEdit; **123** (br) ©Masterfile; **124** ATTILA KISBENEDEK/AFP/Getty Images; **139** ©Stockbyte/Alamy Images; **141** (c) Fotosonline/ Alamy; **145** (br) Getty Images/Stockdisc; **145** (tr) © Ed Bohon/CORBIS; **147** (b) ©Photos.com/ JupiterImages; **147** (b) ©Photodisc/Getty Images; **147** (t) ©Skip Nail/Digital Vision/Getty Images; **149** (b) ©Thomas Northcut/Getty Images; **152** (bg) ©Houghton Mifflin Harcourt; (inset) ©Houghton Mifflin Harcourt; **G2** © Adisa/ Shutterstock; **G3** ©Andersen Ross/Photodisc/ Getty Images; **G4** Ryan McVay/Photodisc/Getty Images; **G5** © Getty Images; **G6** © Comstock, Inc./JupiterImages; **G7** C Squared Studios/ Photodisc/Getty Images; **G8** ©PhotoDisc/Getty Images; **G9** © Comstock, Inc./JupiterImages

Illustrations
Cover John Shroades; **4** Raúl Colón; **30–32** Rick Powell; **36–37** Ken Bowser; **42–53** Raúl Colón; **62** Bernard Adnet; **54–65** Ken Bowser; **98–109** (art background) Ken Bowser; **115–116** (props) Pamela Thompson; **114–116** Bob Barner; **118** Bernard Adnet; **126–137** Russell Benfanti; **142–144** Claudine Gevry.

All other photos: Houghton Mifflin Harcourt Photo Libraries and Photographers.